Making Time to Change the World

Making Time to Change the World

A Student Handbook for Engaging in Service

KENT SCHIETINGER *and* GRANT SCHIETINGER

Archway Publishing books may be ordered through booksellers or by contacting:

Archway Publishing
1663 Liberty Drive
Bloomington, IN 47403
www.archwaypublishing.com
1 (888) 242-5904

ISBN: 978-1-4808-6089-6 (sc)
ISBN: 978-1-4808-6090-2 (e)

Library of Congress Control Number: 2018903470

Print information available on the last page.

Archway Publishing rev. date: 05/09/2018

Contents

"Plant trees under whose shade you may never sit."

~ *Nelson Henderson*

This book is dedicated to all those people, known and unknown, who have given some of their time to making a positive difference in the world. We hope it will inspire others to act.

All profits from the sale of this book will be donated to charity.

Introduction

Life sometimes plops opportunity into your lap and you are left with the decision to act on it or spend time and energy on other things. Our specific journey into service was unexpected and when we began, we had no idea where we would wind up. We will talk about that later in this book, but first we want to explain why we are writing this instead of spending all of our free time doing those things that teenagers like to do.

We are writing this book for you, not us. There is nothing we gain (except royalties, fame and maybe a spot on the *Today* show). Seriously, though, this book is intended to inspire people. It is a message to people of all ages, but particularly teens and even those of you on the cusp of the teen years. It's not a call to action, but rather encouragement to act. It's our story from beginning to end and the message that everything that we and you do has an impact on others. Understanding the power that we each possess to change the world is the first step in getting involved. After that, knowing how to seek out and handle the vast opportunities that exist for service are the keys to your success.

So, we will now answer the question that every college interviewer asked us: "What does the title really mean?" Actually, that question makes more sense if you understand that our original title referenced a video game system that we love to play (one word, two syllables, four letters) and was, "Leaving [name of game system] to Change the World." We have spent many, many hours playing that game, imagining ourselves to be Major League Baseball players, champions on the soccer and football fields, and sharpshooters. Some of our biggest arguments have resulted from the fact that when twins play each other, one is sure to lose. Those games are as important and engaging to us as they are to hundreds of thousands, maybe millions, of others in America. That's exactly why we felt that it was so important that it be part of the title of this book; but, trademark rules ultimately prevented us from using the game system name. That was ok, though, because our reference to it actually represents far more than the game itself. It represents all the things that people do in their spare time for enjoyment. And, there is nothing wrong with enjoyment! But, we are making the point that taking *some* time away from whatever it is that you like to do, and directing it to service, can actually make a difference in the world. That's how we came up with the current title that you now see on the cover; our real message is about just making time to change the world.

The original title was also a play on the title of a book that left an impression on us. We talk about it in the chapter on role models and the stories that inspired us even before we knew the project we would undertake. That book is *Leaving Microsoft to Change the World*, by John Wood; it tells the story of a guy who "had it all" in corporate America and left it to build schools and libraries in developing nations.

Now we will tell you the specifics of what this book is about and hopefully you'll keep reading! You should know that even if your teacher or guidance counselor or parents make you read it, we think that by the end you will be glad you did. And, it could really change your life, not to mention the lives of others.

We already told you that this book is meant to inspire you. But, what good is inspiration if you are left with enthusiasm to do something positive and have no idea how to find a project or how to carry one out. We came upon our project by chance and, actually, we were not even looking for one. After we began to work on it, we had the encouragement of a lot of people, but ultimately were left to figure out the path to our goal on our own. Some of what had to be done was obvious, like taking money out of our savings to buy bulk candy and water at Costco and selling it at exorbitant prices at school and community events to raise money. Other things, though, like writing grant proposals, needed a lot of research. Even finding out who to send the proposals to was a chore in itself. So, think of this book as a blueprint or guide map for service. Because our project involved large-scale fundraising, we will talk specifically about that, but there are many types of other projects we will address, as well. We are pretty confident that you can take the information we provide and easily adapt it to whatever direction you decide to go.

So, in a nutshell, after we do our best to inspire you, we will tell you how to carry out your plan. Along the way, we will try to entertain you a bit so you'll keep reading instead of tossing the book aside, and going back to your favorite game system or whatever else you love to do in your spare time.

How We Came To Service

Remember we told you that we are typical teenagers? We will keep driving that point home, not because we are trying to convince ourselves, but because you need to know how much like you we are. If there is a stereotype that service is an activity only of certain types of people, that's wrong. Sometimes teens think doing service is not cool or best left for a certain type of kid. Toss that idea out the window. Service is very "cool" and all types of people, even the "coolest" people among you, can and should and do get involved.

Service was always part of our lives growing up. Our parents were not in the Peace Corps or anything like that (though how cool would that have been!), but they were involved in a project that they started when we were really young and continue with today. Here is the story we have been told many times.

When we were babies, and our older brother was about two-years old, there was an article in *The New York Times* about the war in Sudan. Apparently, there was a photo on the front page of kids hiding behind a tree and the story of how families were being torn apart and children were left to witness horrific crimes and be killed or die trying to flee to safety. Our dad asked our mother if she thought they could adopt a child and she said "no," because they already had three kids under three-years old and she was a working mom. But, she said she believed she and our dad could still figure out how to help in some way. Now, here is the part of the story that should inspire you to be creative about how you find service projects and approach carrying them out. We will revisit that idea later, as well.

Our dad always loved basketball. He came from a Division I college and was an avid fan of the sport. In the course of his research about the kids he wanted to help, he learned that Sudan, and its Dinka tribe, produced some of the tallest people in the world. He then also researched athletes that had come from Sudan and identified some names he recognized and others who were not known to him, but who he was able to track down. He came up with an idea that he could raise a relatively small amount of money to bring potentially talented athletes from Sudan to America and get them scholarships at prep schools where they could hone their basketball skills and study, then be able to go on to get athletic scholarships in college. He made a few connections, one with a Sudanese man who had played basketball in Europe and now resides in the United States, and another with a professional scout from Cameroon who made his own education at Georgetown possible through basketball in the 1980s. Our dad then told as many people as he knew about the plan and, in no time at all, young athletes were being brought to America. The two men from Africa that he had connected with made the trips to find the kids and they, with our dad, located the schools that would take them. We remember dad telling us that selling the idea to schools was difficult at first; but, after the first few kids came and word got out about the project, schools were lining up to take the kids. In fact, the first school said it would need our dad to pay partial tuition, which was not how the plan was supposed to go; but, he said he would figure out how to do that and the kids were placed there. Within months, the school was so impressed with the kids that they called to say no more money would be needed.

Here is the beauty of the project. If our mother had said "yes" and our parents had adopted a child from Africa, the impact (aside from one of us having to share our bedroom) would have been that one life would have been bettered, maybe even saved. But, by doing what they did instead, they have affected many lives. To date, they have been involved in bringing to America over 100 kids, all of whom have gotten excellent high school and college educations.

They have graduated, or will graduate, from some of the top schools in the country, including Georgetown, Amherst, Notre Dame and Harvard. It costs a few thousand dollars to bring each kid here, which is a fairly small amount when you consider what the outcome is. Our dad's theory was that by making a small dollar investment, keyed to a larger plan, he and my mom could help far more kids than simply focusing on one and the cost that it would have required to raise and educate him or her. Then, those kids who were helped would go on to help others, whether as professional athletes or in more traditional fields that they became qualified to enter because of the great educations they received. The point is, they would have the skills and the opportunity to be successful and then use their success to help better the world. And that's how it has worked.

The other great part about this project that our parents were involved in is that everyone has benefited from it. Our parents and other financial donors have the satisfaction of knowing that they truly are helping others. The kids who participate get the benefit of a life changed by education and a chance for success in America. The schools that give these kids scholarships not only have the distinction of doing something benevolent, but also get great athletes who contribute to their programs. Also, the kids who come over are amazing people; they enrich the student bodies at their schools and work incredibly hard because they realize the opportunity that they have been given. One kid was at one of the top Ivies, majoring in engineering, and had the highest GPA on the team. Consider what talent likely would have been wasted if he had not been part of this service project.

So, the two of us watched this going on over the course of many years and just assumed that service was what everyone does. We also had the benefit of meeting several of these African kids. Although, they at first came from Sudan, the search later expanded to the Congo, Cameroon, Nigeria, Gabon and other parts of Africa. That meant we grew up with "friends" from all over the continent. Even when we were too young to understand our parents' project, we were fascinated by our visitors as they stopped at our house on the way to their schools or spent a vacation with us. One had spent eight years as an indentured servant in Egypt, where his family sent him for safety. Another picked up our brother's guitar and played a perfect rendition of "Stairway to Heaven" that he learned in a refugee camp. We marveled at their seven-foot plus frames and their stories from back home. They enriched our lives as much as we enriched theirs. The experience also made us understand the power we all have to make a difference in the lives of others and in the world.

That has been our parents' biggest service project, by far, but not the only one. While our dad was trying to change the world, our mom was always doing something to help the local community. She ran events for this or that charity or volunteered for various projects. She also helped us start a youth group when our older brother was in 8th grade and we were in 6th. It was through a not-for-profit organization, People to People, International (PTPI), and was chartered as one of its local chapters. She said it would be a good way to get other students involved and provide some structure for our service activities. We raised money for Heifer International and for communities devastated by natural disasters in various parts of the world. We found a solar flashlight company that would donate one flashlight to a developing country for each flashlight we sold in the U.S. We also started two annual projects that continued until we all went off to college. One was a holiday book drive and the other was a food, coat and winter clothes drive for a New York City soup kitchen.

Now, in case you are thinking we must have spent all of our free time doing this charity work and are lying about playing sports and having a social life, you're completely wrong. Part of the point of telling you all this is to show you how people have really busy and complete lives, yet manage to fit service in, and do so in a pretty big way. The book drive ran in the month of November each year. We got the idea for it when we started talking about getting rid of our old children's books, many of which were brand new, and wondering where we could donate them. Then we read a newspaper article about the neediest families in New York City and how so many people would not get any presents for the holidays. So, we thought why not collect and donate books in time for Christmas. We put bins at the local schools, libraries and stores, asking for donations, and publicized the project through the local newspaper and flyers. We collected thousands of books! We then sorted them by condition and reading levels, and located a charity to distribute them. For many people, they were the only holiday gifts they received.

We found out about the soup kitchen from one of our mother's co-workers who volunteered there. Many food bank programs do not want volunteers under eighteen years old, but this one welcomed us. So, every few months we would volunteer on a Saturday morning and help prepare and serve the food. It was hard to not be moved by the people we met. Then, we got the idea to collect gently used coats and warm clothes for the winter since some of the population served was homeless. We also collected canned foods. Again, the donations poured in and the impact they made on the lives of the needy was great.

So, that's how we came to service. For us, it was a part of our lives, but for many of the friends whom we got to help, it was their first time getting involved. The point is that everyone needs to start someplace and the opportunities, through a group or from your own ideas, are all around you. There is a lot of need out there; you just have to notice it and take the first step. Our really big project, which we'll tell you about shortly, literally fell into our laps (or, we should say, our lacrosse sticks). First, though, a word about role models.

2

Looking For Inspiration? There Are Role Models All Around

*O*ddly enough, we never really stopped to think of our parents as service role models to us. They were more general role models and their influence kind of seeped into us in the course of growing up. They also had us believing that helping others was just something that you did naturally. But, there were some other people whom we learned about over the years who blew us away with their commitment to helping those in need. We are pretty sure that if you hear their stories, you'll also be moved to get involved and become inspired to believe that you can, in fact, make a difference. You may actually have heard of others who inspire you, since there are millions of people who dedicate all or part of their lives to making the world a better place. These are just our four favorites and they operate on very different levels, which is another important idea to understand.

Bill and Melinda Gates

So, we all know Bill Gates as the co-founder of Microsoft and its billionaire CEO and Chairman. Yes, he is crazy wealthy, having a fortune equal to $1.5 billion more than the GDP of Iceland. And, yes, he is in a better position than most people to help those in need. But, before you skip down the page to find someone more like yourself, ask yourself if you know exactly what he has done and how he has done it. The quick answer is that he has not just thrown his money at projects; he and his wife, Melinda, have made service a significant part of their lives and the scope of his work should be inspiring to everyone.

The Bill & Melinda Gates Foundation is one of the largest private foundations in the world. Its goals are, globally, to enhance healthcare and reduce extreme poverty and, in America, to expand educational opportunities and access to information technology. Bill and Melinda have said that their service is motivated by the belief that every life has equal value and all people should have the opportunity to lead healthy, productive lives. In developing countries, their focus is on improving people's health and giving them the chance to lift themselves out of hunger and extreme poverty. In the United States, they seek to ensure that all people, especially the most underprivileged, have access to the opportunities people need to succeed in school and life.

So, the reason we picked Bill and Melinda Gates for our short honor role of those who inspire us is because they have chosen to dedicate a huge part of their lives and their fortunes to service. There are many others like them who are worthy of mention, but our short book limits those whom we can include. The two that we discuss next have worked with fewer resources and gotten less acclaim, but each made an impact on us, for reasons you will read about, and motivated us to roll up our sleeves and get involved in something bigger than ourselves.

John Wood

John Wood was an executive at Microsoft. In 1988, he took a vacation to trek through the Himalayas. On his journey, he met a person from the Annapurna Circuit of Nepal who was involved with the local schools and took him to visit one. There were 450 children and only a few books, most of which were romance novels and other writing that was not age appropriate or educationally useful. Wood has said that he was shocked to find a school with no books and has reported that the school's headmaster told him, "Perhaps, sir, you will someday come back with books." Wood took the suggestion, went to an Internet café in Katmandu, and asked friends and relatives for donations. One year later, he returned to the school with 3,000 books. Soon after that experience, he decided to leave Microsoft and devote his life full-time to a project called, "Books for Nepal." It was the beginning of a larger foundation he would form called, "Room to Read." This global organization focuses on literacy and gender equality in education and operates in ten countries in Asia and Africa, serving more than 8.8 million children. As of 2016, Room to Read had established over 1,850 schools and 16,800 libraries, distributed 18 million books, and published over 1,300 local-language children's books. In addition, it has helped more than 28,000 girls through its long-term girls' education program and reached 11.6 million children worldwide. When we graduated from 6th grade, our parents gave us a copy of the book that Wood's wrote of his journey into service, along with a few other more meaningful gifts, like a new video game system and some games. They said the book was on behalf of our African friends and borrowed for the inscription, the mantra of Room to Read: "World change starts with educated children." The name of his book is *Leaving Microsoft to Change the World*, the inspiration for our own.

Kevin Dugan

Our third role model is likely someone you have not heard about. He is a former Division I lacrosse player and coach. His name is Kevin Dugan and his charity is Fields of Growth (FoG). His work has dramatically changed the course of the future for a village in Uganda and altered the lives of its inhabitants. His website quotes the following words of Howard Thurman, an African American civil rights leader who inspired him: "Don't ask yourself what the world needs; ask yourself what makes you come alive. And then go and do that. Because what the world needs is people who have come alive."

Coach Dugan is a 2001 graduate of the University of Notre Dame and a former member of the Fighting Irish Men's Lacrosse Team. After graduation, he went on to get an MBA at Wheeling Jesuit University, where he served as an assistant coach for two seasons. A former finance major, he had a brief stint at Merrill Lynch before going on to coach college lacrosse for six seasons. He made stops at Gordon, Yale and Scranton before spending two years as the Director of Operations for Notre Dame's program.

Coach Dugan is the benefactor of The Hopeful Village in Uganda, located about four hours from the capital of Kampala. His efforts began there while he was the Head Men's Lacrosse Coach at the University of Scranton. As a leader in the university's international service program, he travelled to El Salvador, Ecuador, Jamaica and Uganda. Around the same time, he became involved with the Federation of International Lacrosse (FIL) and was being sent around the world to consult with the Federation's newest member nations.

The path of service that he has taken is not hard to chart. His work in international service and his travels with the Federation of International Lacrosse led to the intersection of three passions – leadership, service and lacrosse. Embracing these three core commitments, in 2009 he founded Fields of Growth. Within a few years, the New Jersey native committed himself to running the organization, while also working with the Federation of International Lacrosse to advance its mission to bring lacrosse to the Olympics.

Fields of Growth aims to harness the passion of the lacrosse community into positive social impact through global leadership, service and growing the game. For Coach Dugan, like John Wood, service and social change became the main focus of their lives.

✿ ✿ ✿

So, those are four of the people whom we admire because they have dedicated their lives to helping others. As we said at the beginning of this chapter, though, there are people all around you who may inspire you. Change can happen quickly or slowly and can come about in big or small ways. The four people we present here have taken very different approaches to service, yet each has made a huge impact. The point is to recognize that there are a lot of paths to service, to choose one for yourself, and then to get up and take action.

3

A Funny Thing Happened On The Way To Lacrosse Practice (or, Projects Come From The Most Unexpected Places)

So, if you are thinking that you might be interested in service, but can't figure out a project for yourself to get involved in, don't worry. Just the fact that you are inclined to do something is a great step. This chapter will tell you how we came upon our most significant service project and then will give you some project ideas you can follow up on. The fact is that there are service opportunities all around you and all you have to do is give it some thought and seek out those projects that you think will interest you the most.

Before we came upon our idea for our "big" project, which was fundraising to build a school in Uganda, we had pursued a number of small projects through the youth group we started under People to People. People to People is a not-for-profit organization that was founded in 1956 by President Dwight D. Eisenhower. It promotes international understanding and friendship through educational, cultural and humanitarian activities. We used the umbrella of People to People to form our youth group, called a PTPI Chapter by the parent organization, because it gave us some structure and incentive to keep our group active in various activities. It also helped us as we set out on projects, to have a parent organization that gave us some legitimacy in terms of dealing with the press and the public. In the final chapter of this book, we tell you more about forming a PTPI Chapter. For now, People to People is mentioned for its role as the organization through which we pursued a number of "smaller" service projects during our middle school and high school years.

The best way to come up with service ideas is to ask a lot of people for input. In our youth group, we would regularly ask members what suggestions they had for upcoming service projects. One person suggested Heifer International. That organization was founded by a man named Dan West, who was a farmer from the Midwest and went to the Spanish Civil War as an aide worker. As he distributed the rationed one cup of milk a day to refugees, he thought that giving them a cow, instead of a cup, would change their lives. So, close to 70 years ago he founded an organization that would provide people with the means to sustain themselves, rather than to be dependent on charity throughout their lives. Through cash donations, his organization gives people animals to produce food and income from products such as milk, eggs and honey. So, our group collected money that was used by the organization to change impoverished communities and assist families throughout the world.

Another member of our group heard of a solar flashlight company that was willing to donate one flashlight for every flashlight sold; through that we were able to send flashlights to Third World countries. We got feedback that women and children were using them to walk in the night to outhouses or back from school and work. One letter even said that the lights were allowing emergency medical services to be provided in the darkness.

Another member, inspired by Room to Read, which we told you about in the last chapter, suggested a used book drive and we annually collected hundreds of books that we sorted and delivered to needy families in time for the holidays in December, providing what to many was the only gift they would receive. Then we heard about a soup kitchen in New York City near Harlem and we asked if we could volunteer. After our first visit we decided we could help more if we collected canned goods and clothing, so at various times throughout the year that became our group's primary project.

Those are just a few examples of the types of service you can get involved in. Talk to people, read newspapers and magazines, search the Internet and just think for a few minutes about the people or places that you think could use some help. There are possibilities all around you. Remember the story we told you about our parents? Their service came from reading the newspaper one Sunday morning in our kitchen. Just keep your eyes and ears and imaginations open and ideas will come to you.

Sometimes, however, service opportunities will come when you least expect them. Here's the story of our biggest project.

From the time we were very young, we both played lacrosse. By middle school, it was often all we could think of. Grant would spend hours of his free time on the Internet, combing through lacrosse websites. He followed all the college players and coaches and knew just about everything there was to know about the game and what was going on around it. One day when he was in 5th grade, he found an article online about a college coach who was teaching kids in Uganda to play lacrosse. It was Coach Dugan, whom we wrote about in the last chapter. At the time, he was the Head Men's Lacrosse Coach at Scranton, a Division I program in the Northeast. Coach Dugan had founded his organization, Fields of Growth, and was teaching kids in the Hopeful Village to play a game that he was passionate about. In fact, he spent most of his free time in Uganda transforming the lives of these kids through the sport he loves.

When Grant saw the article, he immediately thought about the work that our parents had done, at that point, for about ten years. He emailed Coach Dugan and told him that he should talk to our dad since they both were working to help kids in Africa have a better life. He also told me about it and we passed on the information to our parents. Then, we did one other thing. The article mentioned that the organization was always in need of lacrosse equipment. We emailed Coach Dugan a second time and told him that we would collect used equipment from teams and players on Long Island, where we lived, and clean it up for the kids in Uganda to use. Coach

Dugan's response was enthusiastic and he was all too happy to have some help with his project.

The next year was spent visiting youth lacrosse teams across Long Island to ask players to donate used equipment. Lacrosse is a huge sport on the island, so it was fairly easy to get donations. The real trick was collecting the equipment, cleaning it, sorting it by size/age, and bundling it for shipment to Africa. That last point was possibly the biggest hurdle since the cost of shipping is significant. Donations were solicited and many times Coach Dugan carried bags with him on trips to Africa from the U.S.

That, it would turn out, was not our biggest project with Coach Dugan, however. This is where the title of this chapter, "Projects Come From The Most Unexpected Places," comes in.

We worked out with a lot of the college players when they were home on school breaks and we had become friendly with them. Sometime even if they weren't working out with us, they would still stop by our house to say hello when they were on Long Island. Some of these same players were spending school breaks in Uganda with Coach Dugan doing service work and, of course, helping him teach the local kids lacrosse. One of these college guys, a player for UNC Chapel Hill, was visiting us at the end of August just before we were to start 7th grade. After we had a lacrosse catch, we were in our kitchen and we asked him about what he did on his service trip. He said he helped repair the school there. He went on to explain that it was made of mud, cardboard and cloth. Shocked, we asked him what he was talking about and he repeated what he had said about the school. He then showed us a picture and we couldn't believe what we were seeing. It could not even be described as a tent because it was not nearly that complete. This "school" was a mess of scraps pasted together with mud. It was a disgrace. Yet, next to it were about a dozen kids, probably age three to twelve, with wide smiles on their faces. Some had tattered shorts and t-shirts; others had worn, dirty hand-me-down school uniforms. All of them were barefoot. But, most startling was this "school." Out loud, one of us said to our college lacrosse friend, "How can that be a school? How can anyone learn in a place like that?"

At that point our mom came into the kitchen and we showed her the picture. Like us, she was shocked and also saddened by what she saw. Then came the next big shock. Our lacrosse friend said it was really a shame that the school was in such a terrible state since only $20,000 in U.S. money could build a permanent school made of cinderblock. We were stopped in our tracks. What? That money was a teenager's car in our town. It was a small addition to someone's house. Maybe it was a few nice vacations. If that was all that was needed to build a school for these kids, then why the heck hadn't anyone done it?

Then and there, on a warm summer afternoon, standing in our kitchen, we decided to take on a project half way around the world that would consume the next five years and change not only our lives, but the lives of hundreds of kids whom we might never meet. When we told our mom that we would raise the funds, she said that she thought that would be a great project for us to focus on. She pointed out that it actually is a large amount of money to raise, but said it is a great cause and we would not only learn a lot in the process, but could seriously change people's lives.

That night we talked about it some more between ourselves and then with both of our parents. We remember our mom telling our dad that if we were going to do it, it had to be our own effort; we'd have to succeed or fail on our own. So, our parents said they would stay out of it because it would have far less value to us if they simply wrote a check or orchestrated the donations. "We'll let you give it a shot and let's see how far you can take it," they said.

That evening we emailed Coach Dugan and told him we would raise the money to construct the school. He was thrilled to hear of the plan and said he would support us in any way he could.

So began our project to build a school in Uganda.

4

The First Steps: Putting Your Project Down On Paper And Out In Public

As you come up with an idea for a project, it is important to really think out your plan. Taking some time before you jump into action will actually save you time in the long run; it may even be the difference between success and failure. Planning will not only help you sort out the different approaches you will take, but it will also identify your targets and a time frame for reaching your goals. So, grab a notebook and a pen and start thinking! And when we say "notebook," we are being literal. If you have one readily identifiable place where all of your project information is located, it will be much easier for you to organize your efforts. A notebook with pockets or a pocket folder is also important.

The first step is to write out a plan. This is the nuts and bolts outline of what you want to accomplish and how you think you will go about it.

Identify the beneficiary of your work

If you are working with or for the benefit of an organization, talk with its leaders before you spend a lot of time on the planning stage. There are many projects you can do on your own, such as a used book or coat drive, but even with those you will need to identify a place that is willing to take what you collect. It will also help you get donors if you can identify a specific beneficiary because it lets people know that whatever they give you will be put to a specific, well-thought-out use. It will also avoid a snag in the project down the road. In fact, here is a story that illustrates that last point.

The second year of our book drive, we were all set to give our thousands of books to the same charity that took them the first year. It was a Brooklyn-based organization that serves approximately 10,000 very needy families in and around New York City. They had both a truck to pick up the books from our house after they were collected and sorted, and a means in place for their distribution. The next year, however, once our garage was packed with collected books, when we contacted the charity to arrange a pick up, we were told that because of a bed bug outbreak in New York and its boroughs, they were not allowed to take any donations, other than cash, until further notice. We were in a bit of a panic. Our parents wanted the garage cleaned out and it was loaded with 4,000 books. In the end, it was fine; we asked each member of our youth group to be responsible for distributing 200 books and many organizations were incredibly happy to receive them. But, if we had bothered to check with our first charity before we began the collection in the second year, we could have planned otherwise from the start.

In the case of our school project, the beneficiary was easy for us to identify since The Hopeful School itself was the inspiration. More often, you will get an idea for a project and then have to look for the organization or group that will receive the product of your efforts. The good news is that there are charities all around us that need help. At the back of this book, in the "Resources" chapter, are some places or causes you might consider.

Create a blueprint

For a builder, a blueprint outlines what the project will look like and guides him or her through the process of constructing it. The same is true of your plan for a service project.

For our school project, we knew that the goal was to build a school in Uganda. We knew from our discussions with Fields of

Growth that the facility had to house about 250 students. And, we knew that we needed $20,000 in U.S. money to fund the construction.

An important part of the process of creating your blueprint is knowing what you do NOT need to focus on. Without thinking this through in advance, you run the risk of wasting time on tasks that do not have to be done. For example, if you have a coat drive and know that the collection will be donated to the XYZ Homeless Shelter, and they have told you, in advance, that they are happy to accept it, you do not need to spend time looking for recipients of the coats you collect. If the beneficiary is an organization and it has a truck, like our book charity did, you do not need to figure out how you will transport the goods. For our school project, we knew that we did not need to worry about who would do the construction of the school building, since Fields of Growth was taking care of that through volunteers. We also knew we did not need to worry about getting supplies to, or in, Uganda, because that, too, was covered. The narrower your focus is, the better chance you have of completing the project. If there are several components to it, then compartmentalize each of those and focus on them in order of what makes most sense to do first, then move to the second thing, etc.

Once you know what you are going to do, plan out how you will do it. This is where your blueprint gets a little more detailed. Start by brainstorming. Write down everything you can imagine as a way to approach your goal. This is not the time for fine-tuning; that will come later. At this point you want to record every single reasonable idea that you have on how to accomplish what you are setting out to do. Since many service projects involve collecting something, whether that is money or clothing or food or something else, jot down all the ideas you have on how you will do that. If your service project involves only donating your own time, such as working as a literacy volunteer or helping in a soup kitchen, then make a big stick figure of yourself and move onto thinking about where and how you would like to lend a hand.

The brainstorming part of your planning is where you should

let your imagination run wild. Remember, this is your planning notebook; you don't have to let anyone see it. So, be sure to put on paper your common sense ideas, as well as those which are unlikely. Sure, you probably will not get Angelina Jolie to do a public service announcement for you, but you never know. Simply, put down EVERYTHING you can think of.

Now, come back down to Earth. Sorry, but you have a lot of work to do, after all. But, don't throw away those ideas that are unlikely to happen. Once you have gotten your project going and you are doing, or have done, all the "nuts and bolts" work, you should come back to your dream page and you might just by then have the time and the enthusiasm to pursue one or two long shots. For now, though, at this stage when your project is still just a vision, you're going to focus on the more practical ideas to get the project off the ground. For us, this meant figuring out the most likely ways to get money relatively quickly. Those last words, "relatively quickly," are important to be aware of.

Some things you do will bring about faster results than others and a good project has both components. For example, if you want to save the planet, that's going to take some time. Your "long run" effort can be focused on working with lawmakers to get laws that will assist you in your goal. Your "short run" effort is something more like organizing a recycling drive. If your project involves collecting money, as ours did, then it is important to realize that you will need some "short run" ideas so you can start getting donations quickly and get your project underway. On the other hand, "long run" ideas will often bring bigger results, so you have to plant the seeds and watch them grow. A good example is a grant or a big corporate donation. Each of those require a process that is going to take some time before you have a result. We talk more about "long run" and "short run" ideas in the next section.

So, now is the time to go through your more practical ideas and figure out what you are going to pursue. You may wind up pursuing all of them, but putting them in the order in which you will do them will help you with organization. After each one that you list, write down anyone you might ask to help you, what "tools" you will need, and basically the mechanics of how you plan to get it done. If you are going to need publicity, write that down. If you will need a banner, write that down. If you will need collection bins, write that down. If you will need a driver and you don't have a license, write that down. Even if you are wrong and don't wind up needing something, it is better that you wrote it down because at least you will know that you thought of it and it is one less snag you have to worry about later.

Identify your donors

Many projects involve donors. Certainly, ours did. We have written a separate section about donors, not in recognition of all they give, but because they are such a big part of so many service activities.

For us, our donors were going to be the lifeblood of The Hopeful School. Our goal was money, and lots of it. Aside from the fundraising activities we planned, donations from people, organizations and other groups were crucial, so we set aside a whole page in our notebook to identify them. Because our project dealt with soliciting money, that is the framework within which we will guide you; however, the same general approach applies to organizing all types of projects.

When you are dealing with donors, the categories are "big" and "small." Think about all the individuals or categories of people whom you can ask to help you meet your goal. Think about public figures who might be sympathetic to the cause you are supporting. Think generally about grants and corporate sponsorships. Again, try to think about what sources might have the same inclination as you to help a particular cause. Jot down whatever you come up with and then separate your donors into groups according to how you will approach them. Some donors will be okay with an email, and that is the easiest group to target. Others will need something more formal, like a letter. Still others may want to talk about the project after getting some preliminary information. And, other sources, like corporations or grant providers, will require a formal written approach. We talk more about written solicitations and grants a little later on.

Talk to anyone and everyone

Getting ideas and feedback from others is helpful throughout your project, but it is especially important in the planning stages. Our grandfather used to say that no one has a monopoly on brains, and he was right. As smart as you might be, and as excited as you may feel about the project, getting input from other people, particularly adults, can only help your effort. We talked through our ideas with our parents and Coach Dugan. You might ask a parent or a coach, or maybe a teacher or advisor at school.

Be mindful of what you are asking for. You are not asking someone to figure out your ideas for you. Most adults don't have the time to sit down and plan from scratch something for you to do. Also, you want the project to be your own. So, ask for feedback after you have worked out your plan and made your blueprint. Make sure they understand that you would like them to comment on what you have and give you additional ideas, but not take responsibility for designing a course for you to follow.

Now, if you bother to ask for feedback, there are two other things you must be prepared to do. First, listen carefully and make the effort to take notes. If you value someone's suggestions and ideas, you will want to be sure that you can remember them after you meet so that you can consider acting on them; it would be a bad idea to have to call someone back because you couldn't remember what he or she said. Second, don't be upset if the person you ask for feedback thinks that some of your ideas won't work or could be done a better way. If you really want feedback (and you should), then you have to be prepared for some constructive criticism. And, once you get it, you should consider it because it may actually improve upon your idea. You know the saying: "Two heads are better than one."

Along with getting input from others, telling people your idea will publicize it. You never know if someone knows another person who can help you in a big way. Or, someone you never expected to get a donation from may just have a soft spot for what you are trying to do. Here is a great illustration of how we experienced this with our school project. One day we were sitting at our kitchen table with someone who helped our mom with errands and her sister who was a year younger than us. We had the letters on the school project on the table near where the sister was sitting. She asked what the project was about and we told her. When we were done talking, she said, "I'll give you $500." We thought she was kidding, but she said she was serious and wanted to help. She then went on to explain that she had saved money from her birthday and Christmas to buy two front section tickets to a concert at Madison Square Garden in New York City. She said she would rather give the money to the school. We told her to think it over and talk to her mom about it; a few days later we got a $500 check.

A similar situation happened during a school trip. A mother overheard our mother talking about the project and asked for more information. When we explained what we were trying to do, she said she would give us a $250 donation and would tell her friends about it. By the next day we had $350 more.

So, telling as many people as you can—everyone you meet, in fact—will do nothing but help you. No matter how many donors you identify on your own, there are always more that you never even thought of. And you never know who knows someone else. In these days of social media, publicizing things is even easier, so make sure you get your story out.

A word about deadlines

You might have noticed that we did not put into the section on creating a blueprint, any reference to deadlines. That's because a deadline is a tricky thing. Some of your projects will have natural deadlines. For example, if you are collecting books to distribute before Christmas, a few weeks before Christmas is the logical deadline. If you are collecting winter clothes, you will want to get them distributed earlier in the season than later so they are most useful.

With our school project, we didn't really have a deadline. We just wanted to collect the money as quickly as possible and understood that the majority of it would come in bits and pieces. But, we didn't realize the project was going to take more than five years. And that brings us to our point about deadlines.

The tricky thing about deadlines is that if you don't know realistically how to set them, and you then miss them, it can discourage you and might ruin your project. Think about how we would have felt if we expected our school project to be done in six months and by that point had only collected a few thousand dollars. Or worse, think about how disheartened Coach Dugan would have been if he expected the money in a few months. The point is that you might not understand how long a project may take and if you commit to something that turns out to be too difficult to work with, someone's likely to be disappointed. Fortunately, we did not put a deadline on our project. We just said we would do it until we hit our goal. And then we just kept going.

5

Putting Your Plans Into Action

Written solicitations

The easiest way to solicit is to do it in writing. That gives you the opportunity to put all your points down and edit your pitch as many times as you need to in order to present your proposal coherently. It also gives recipients a chance to process what you are trying to do. It is far more realistic to expect a large donation from a letter than from a verbal pitch, which is likely to be a bit disorganized and hindered by nervousness. Be prepared, though, that some people also may want to speak with you after they receive and consider your letter. That's okay; the process of putting your ideas down in writing will help you prepare for that, too.

So, our first task was to write a letter soliciting donations. We sat down and together drafted something that explained our project, our goal and our motivation. You can see this letter in the chapter on "Resources" in the back of this book. When we were done, we sent it to Coach Dugan for him to approve. An important part of working with an organization is getting approval for what you want to do and the authorization to use the organization's name, logo, etc.

Our next step was to identify who would get our letter. The advantage of email is that you can do mass mailings for free and relatively easily. We decided to send the letter to EVERYONE we had ever met, as well as everyone our parents knew. So, first we made up a quick list of categories of people. It looked like this:

People
Teachers (go back all the way and include anyone you had a good relationship with)
Principals
Coaches (in school and out of school)
Advisors (youth groups, special projects, etc.)
Our friends' parents
Our parents' friends
Our parents' colleagues
Neighbors
Relatives
People in the community (from your school contact lists and community leaders)

Groups
Local Girl Scout and Boy Scout troops and other community groups
Church groups
Sports team little league "franchises"
Youth groups

Organizations, Corporations and Public Figures
Identify general service-based not-for-profit organizations (like People to People)
Identify general corporate foundations
Identify specific organizations or people who have a shared interest with your project

Our "people" category was extensive. Our first mailing was more than 1,000 emails. This we accomplished with only our own and our parents' email contact lists. We used the topic, "Service Project – Please Read," and then followed with a brief note asking that the recipient read the attached document about a project that was very important to us. The response was overwhelming. We then went through the school address books for as many years as our mom had kept them and highlighted the people who were not covered by our email contact lists. Because the address books had email addresses, we sent the letters out that way, as well. When we didn't have email addresses (and could not find them anywhere), we mailed letters. Money out of our savings accounts paid for the photocopying and the postage. Where we could hand-deliver the letters (for example, to neighbors or some of our parents' colleagues who were not on an email list), we did that to save costs.

For groups, organizations and corporations, a mailed letter is better than an email because it is more likely to be received. A lot of emailed material that is not sent to a specific person or that arrives from an unknown sender winds up in the trash. You can usually get a mail address online and often can find the name of a person to send your letter to. Even if it is not the correct person, a specifically addressed piece of mail is more likely to be noticed. You can even add a line that says, "If you are not the correct person to handle this request, please forward it to that individual." Remember that when you are asking for a favor, effort and politeness go a long way!

When you are looking for donations from organizations, corporations and public figures, don't be afraid to cast a wide net. The worst someone can do is say "no," so what's the risk? By including as many people in your project as possible, you have a greater chance to succeed.

If you are stuck for ideas, go online and search. For our project, we searched "organizations that support education" and "organizations that help build schools." Remember that before the Internet, it was much harder to get projects done. Now, all you have to do is be creative and potential donors will flood in.

Once you have emailed, delivered or mailed out all of your letters, be prepared for pretty quick responses. By the end of our project we had sent out, one way or another, more than 1,500 letters and communications, and the vast majority of those were responded to. Almost immediately you have to be prepared to do some follow-up.

Managing what you have started

Before you send out a single letter or email, be prepared for what comes next. Here is a quick list:

1. Prepare for questions from people who want more information.

This may involve another letter, a short email response, or a visit to a potential donor. Whatever they ask for, you need to try to deliver. Remember, you want something from them and money or possessions are important to everyone. So, know your letter and know your facts. Emails are relatively easy to respond to. If you get a call and it is not a good time for you to speak, ask if you can call back and set a time to do that. If a local potential donor wants a meeting, have a calendar with your schedule ready and set a time and date, then confirm it in an email.

Now, we will point out that the vast majority of people who gave to our project did not want more information. They got our letter and some may have checked out the website for Fields of Growth, but few contacted us directly other than to send in donations. There was one exception that stands out in our minds, though.

We sent an email to a colleague of our dad who mentioned our project to a very wealthy man who had supported children's charities in the past. We got an email from the man saying he was considering making a donation and would like more information. He wanted to have a telephone conference, so we emailed him some days and times that were available and prepared to speak to him. He kind of made up for all the people who just sent us money, because he had loads of questions. We began by explaining how we came to the school project and what our goal was. He asked us about the village where the school was to be located, the children whom it would serve, how it would be staffed, how we knew the people at Fields of Growth, etc. We could answer most of his questions, but some we could not. So, if we didn't know something, we admitted it and wrote the question down and said we would get back to him. And we did. And he gave us $500.

2. Arrange in advance how you will transmit money.

When you are collecting money, the donations come in pretty quickly, so you have to work out in advance with the beneficiary of your project how you will transmit what you collect. Your letter will tell donors to make checks out directly to the charity. That will avoid you having to handle cash and also give the donors the benefit of a tax deduction. We worked out a system where every Saturday we mailed to Fields of Growth whatever checks we had collected that week. The more difficult situation arises when you collect cash. Some of our projects generated a good amount of change and bills. You don't want to send cash through the mail, so we set up a checking account for our youth group that we could use to avoid that. Most banks will not charge a service fee for an account if you explain that it is for a nonprofit youth group. It also helps if you go to a bank where your parents or some other adult associated with the group does his or her banking. So, as soon as we finished a project that generated cash, we made a deposit in our checking account and then wrote a check from that account to Fields of Growth and sent it in.

3. Get out your notebook and write everything down.

Recordkeeping is very important! In fact, we have a separate section on it a little later on. But, the process of recording your project begins as soon as you finish your blueprint.

Take out that notebook we mentioned earlier and put a tab on a page about halfway into it and make the following chart:

"Donor / Amt. / Cash or Check / Date Rec'd / Date Forwarded / Thank You Sent"

If your project is not collecting money, then modify your headings accordingly. For clothing or book drives, your record keeping may not even be this specific. But, money changes everything. When you are handling money, an incredibly important part of what you do over the next weeks or months or years, will be keeping an up-to-date and accurate record of the money you collect. It will not only let you keep a log of your progress, but it will help you identify what is and what is not working. After a few months, you will be able to look over your chart and see where most of your donations are coming from. You will also be able to go to sleep knowing that everything you have collected is being properly sent and acknowledged. We can't emphasize enough the importance of this part of your project and you will also be perfecting a skill that will benefit you for all of your life.

Following up on unanswered solicitations

There is always the question of when following up on a solicitation is good or when it becomes a bother to people and potentially turns them off. Here there is no set rule; you are going to have to judge what is best to do based on the different situations you are dealing with.

Following up is not a bad thing. Sometimes an email did not reach the intended recipient or sometimes people want to participate and simply get distracted and forget. You can easily check if an email was received and if it was, you generally should not send another if you did not get a response. On the other hand, if it went to someone you are very close with or who expressly asked to be a recipient, then a follow-up is ok. You could say something like, "I just wanted to see if you have any questions about the email I sent you regarding my project." If you do not hear back after that, assume you are not getting a donation and move on.

If you mailed your letter, it is a little trickier. The Post Office says that if you mail something and it is not returned, you can assume that it was delivered. That is hard to believe when that donation check from Uncle Fred never came. Nevertheless, you don't want people to feel harassed and you really do not have the time to follow up on 200 letters. Use the same advice regarding emails that we discuss above; if not having a response from a particular person surprises you, feel free to look into it. There are two exceptions to that advice. If you mailed letters to corporations, feel free to follow up and do so with a telephone call; your letter may never have gotten to the right person. On the other hand, if you hand-delivered letters to your neighbors, rest assured they got them just like they got the Christmas cookies your mom left in their mailboxes. If people did not respond to a hand-delivered letter, assume they are not interested in giving you money and don't embarrass yourself with another solicitation. Now, one time we made an exception to that, but the circumstances were unusual. We had put a letter asking for a donation in a neighbor's mailbox and he never responded. A few months later, his son asked our dad for a donation for his college lacrosse team and our dad gave him a couple hundred dollars, assuming his father had supported our project. When we found out about the situation, we wrote the dad another letter, referencing our father's donation, and forwarded a copy of our original solicitation. He still didn't give us money, but it was worth the effort and might have made him think about making a donation in the future to some other worthy cause.

6

Support Comes From The Most Unexpected Places: Creative Approaches To Project Success

If there is one theme to this chapter, it is creativity. We have mentioned creativity a few times before, but here is another place where it is absolutely important. While your letter writing campaign may bring in the bulk of your donations, you have to attack your project on a number of fronts. Again, our focus here is on fundraising, but creative approaches benefit all types of projects. For our school project, we felt we needed to come up with some fundraising ideas that would bring in donations while our letter solicitations were working in the background.

Now you may be thinking that this is all sounding like a lot of work, between the record-keeping and the letters that you can't just shoot off with an email; but, don't be discouraged. This actually can be the most fun part of a project. It's fun because it lets you think out of the box and engage people as donors rather than just making the request for a contribution. Basically, this is the part where you get to sit down with your partners and think of any wacky way you can get support for your goal (just make sure it's legal, okay?). Seriously, think of all the creative ways that you can have fun and collect donations at the same time. Here are some of the ideas we used to raise funds for our school project.

Change for change

So, how many of you have in your homes those bags or boxes or jars of spare change? We had shoeboxes all over the place brimming with pennies and nickels, dimes and quarters. And how about those cup holders in your cars? It is almost as if people forget that those coins add up to dollars – and a lot of them, at that. So, since people don't want to be burdened by coins, here is a way to take them off their hands. The amazing thing is that The Hopeful School was built, to a large degree, on spare change. Remember that! It's a really important lesson about money.

So, here is what we did. By the way, if you are thinking that you have heard this before, we did mention it earlier in the book, but it is worth mentioning again in a bit more detail.

We took empty five-gallon water jugs and decorated them by pasting 11 inch by 14 inch pieces of paper over their water labels. On those pieces of paper, we typed in large colored letters, "CHANGE FOR CHANGE," and then in smaller letters we explained that we were collecting spare change to help build a school in Uganda. We also taped a cover over the bottle opening and cut a slot into it. We took ten of these decorated bottles and asked permission to put them in supermarkets, train stations, commercial establishments like doughnut shops or diners, banks, schools and business offices. We checked them every few days and when they were at least half full, we emptied them. Now, some people were worried that they might be stolen or emptied, but we had no problem like that. Our biggest problem was carrying the coins and converting them into bills. There are two good solutions to that: invest in a coin converter jar (there are several brands) or find a friend who has an account at a bank that has a coin converter in the lobby. In any event, we are here to tell you that coins do add up and our bottles collected more than $1,000. So, you see, change can surely be used for change.

Doughnuts for change

"Doughnuts" is the generic name we are using to refer to any snack you want to pick; it could be lollipops, gumballs or whatever other snack you can buy cheaply and translate into a big profit. So, we picked doughnuts, those cute little mini ones made out of the doughnut hole to be exact. You can buy a box of 50 for about $9.25. That means you are paying less than 20 cents per piece. We each took a box to school and asked our teachers to put them in the teacher lounge. We also gave our parents boxes to take to work. Each box we distributed had a small card attached that read: "Take a Doughnut, make a donation to charity. Any amount is appreciated." In every case, we got back far more than our original investment. In some cases, we got crazy donations. There were a lot of ten and twenty dollar bills and one person wrote a check for $100.

Sales of food and drinks at school and community events

If there is a big sporting event at school or a town parade, there's an opportunity to make money for your project. Basically, we took $100 from our savings accounts and went to a big bulk store and purchased cases of drinks and boxes of favorite snacks and candy. We then set up a table at an event, made a poster to put on the front of the table, and sold the drinks and snacks at retail prices.

Now there are some important points to keep in mind if you plan on going into the event snack business. First, figure out what you will charge for each drink or snack so that you can make a profit. We charged $1.00 for water, $2.00 for soda or juice, $1.00 for chips and candy. You could also do like we did with our doughnut sale and let people give what they want, but in order to make a profit you may need to set a minimum donation; one mini doughnut costs a lot less than a bottle of water. Also, give some thought to what you will sell. Pizza is a big hit and you could probably charge $3.00 a slice, but it gets cold quickly and then you might be left with unsold pieces.

It's also more expensive than a bulk box of candy bars. If you are selling drinks, people usually like them cold, so consider getting a cooler and ice. You also need to begin with change so you can make change for your customers, so be sure to keep track of that money. Start with something like $20.00 so you can calculate your profits at the end of the day and exclude from that amount the money you started with.

A really important part of the planning for a candy/drink sale is when to do it and where. If your school has a concession stand, you should not go into competition with it. In fact, there may be a whole separate project if you ask the school to donate the concession profits from one event to your project. But, aside from that, you cannot be selling drinks or snacks on school property if the school or a booster club is already doing that. So, check with whatever organization runs concessions; there may be events at times or on days when the stand will be closed. Then all you have to do is get the school's permission to sell on its property. What we did was plan a sale on the day of a town event. For example, if there was a parade in town, we would set up a snack stand on a corner where the parade would pass. The important thing to do here is to get permission from someone to set up your stand. Public property is difficult because technically permits are required. So, we asked the gas station owners on the main road in our town for permission to use the corner of their property. They had no problem with that and for each event we made close to a $100 profit from our sales.

Hire yourself out

This was something we tied in with our youth group, but it can also be done on an individual basis. We had a contest within our group to see who could raise the most money for the Uganda school in one month. Every member was required to bring in at least $100, but the person who collected the most in donations would get a prize. We told everyone that raising the money might be as simple as going door to door and asking ten people for $10 each, but we also talked about doing chores to earn the money, which would make it more interesting. For example, you could do yardwork, or babysit, or tutor, or maybe run errands. There are a lot of possibilities. We distributed flyers listing all the possible services and distributed them to our family friends and neighbors. We found that people were inclined to pay generously if we were willing to put in some effort to help our cause. You can set your own rates or, again, let people give as much as they want.

What didn't work

Some ideas you come up with will not work. Don't be discouraged. If you follow the advice we give you in this section, your failures will be few. Yet, part of learning is learning what does not work, so the lesson is valuable in itself. We will give you an example.

The main idea here is to keep things simple. The fundraisers we outline in this chapter that worked were all clever, but relatively simple. Basically, we didn't have to rely on a lot of people to get them done and there weren't too many moving parts. The one plan that we came up with that failed was way too complicated.

We had an idea to run the longest continuous lacrosse game on record. We planned to attract high school teams and to feature certain coaches, hoping that would encourage their teams and schools to participate. The plan was that in the last few minutes of one game, two new teams would come onto the field so there would be continuous play for more than 30 hours. We would charge an entry fee per team and then charge admission for spectators. We quickly realized, though, that this plan was way too complicated and would take far too much of our time to carry out. Aside from the logistics of recruiting teams, we had to get a venue, a permit, insurance, waiver forms, referees, advertising, volunteers and a sunny day!

It didn't take us long to see that we were getting way out of our league. But, we did learn the value of coming up with simple ideas that could generate profits and that require relatively few hands and little preparation. A good rule of thumb is that if you cannot explain your plan to someone clearly in a few minutes, you should probably think about something else. Do not confuse this, though, with plans that will require more work than going out to buy snacks and selling them to a crowd. Sometimes there is a connection between bigger fundraisers and more money raised. When we say you should keep it simple, that does not mean shy away from work. It means just stick to a simple plan.

✻✻✻

The fundraising ideas that we came up with, and which we discuss in this chapter, should show you how there are many routes to reaching your goal when you take on a service project. What's most important is to come up with simple ideas that will not delay or derail your project. It is also important for you to take charge of your ideas. In every successful project, there has to be a person or a few people who take responsibility for it. Don't plan a snack sale and then have your parents sitting out there at the table. Don't plan anything and then drop the ball. Be prepared to be the last person standing if everyone else bails out and come up with project ideas that will still be successful if that happens. And, remember to have fun. A good rule is to think of what you would participate in if someone else asked for your support.

7

Hunting The Big Game: How To Get Grants And Corporate Donors

Now you may be wondering why we did not discuss grants and corporate donations in the last chapter about support for your project coming from unexpected places. That is because when raising money is your goal, grants and corporate donations can be so important to your project that they deserve discussion all their own. They also form the dividing line between those fundraisers that you may feel comfortable with and those that seem way too complicated and formal. Well, we are here to tell you that getting grants and corporate donations may take a little time at the computer, but the effort can result in large amounts of money for your project. So, this chapter will guide you through the process and give you the tools you need to seek out these big donations. Once you are comfortable in this area, you will use the skills you have learned many times in your life, whether you are raising money for a nonprofit or for yourself to study, travel or promote your career.

First, let's talk about what a grant is. A grant is money or products that are given to an entity, that do not have to be returned or repaid. They come from a "grant maker" which is often a government, trust, foundation or corporation. They are awarded to a recipient, who is usually a business, a nonprofit, an educational program or an individual. Grants are typically given to fund a specific project. Sometimes grants are given to individuals, such as people who are victims of certain events or those who are interested in pursuing a particular course of study or advanced training. Grants sometimes even help small business owners get their businesses off the ground.

Because grants do not need to be repaid, and can provide large donations to a service project, they are great sources to look to for funding. But, they do take a little work to get. In order to be awarded a grant, you have to submit a written proposal or application. This is called "grant writing." Now, stay with us here. Even if this is starting to sound complicated, it's really not; we did it and we are still here to not only talk about it, but to encourage you to do it, as well. The process of grant writing involves explaining your project on an application or submitting a proposal that details what you would do with the money if you were awarded it. You make the submission to a potential funder either on your own initiative or in response to a notice the funder posts that encourages applicants to apply. Now, in this chapter we also speak of corporate donations. Basically, the two forms of funding are the same. Grants may have a more formal process and require some accountability after the grant is awarded, but in both instances you are pitching your idea on paper to a large funding source and getting money for your project that will not have to be repaid.

Before we get into the basics of finding and applying for grants or corporate donations, we should tell you that there are different sizes of grants and corporate donations and there is usually a relationship between the size and the amount of work you need to do to get the award. As you begin your research into available funding, you will see that some grant proposals require far more in the application stage than what suits your project or your time. If you happen to come upon those first, keep looking; we promise that there are grants out there that are relatively simple to secure. Most of the ones you would consider pursuing can be applied for online or in writing via a mailed application.

The first step if you are interested in grants and/or corporate donations is to search the Internet for sources. Search the area in which you are focusing your service project. For example, we searched "grants for education in Africa." You should begin with a narrow search and then broaden it if you want more funding possibilities or you are not finding support for your cause. You could also try a more general search like, "Grants for high school service projects." Almost any words you search under will provide grant sources. In the chapter on "Resources" at the end of this book, we also provide a listing of grant sources you may want to consider.

If you are looking for corporate donors, the process is somewhat the same. We started with the search "corporations that support education," and worked from there. If you know of a few companies that you are interested in, you may want to read about them online to see if they may be likely to support your project even if they have not given donations before to a cause like yours. One of our favorite companies is Patagonia, so when we searched the home site, we saw that the company has a commitment to service. Its focus was different from ours, so we did not solicit a donation, but the few minutes it took to read about the company may have been productive. On the other hand, corporations that are directly tied to education, such as Scholastic, or those like Microsoft, whose founder is dedicated to Africa's plight, were natural points of focus for us. What is important to remember when you are considering corporate donors is that, unlike grant makers, corporations may not advertise that they are giving money away. Here, you are looking for possibilities based on shared interests and you are the one initiating the idea of a corporate donation.

As you search for grants and corporate donors, make a list of five or so that you think may work well for you. Here, you should consider the following:

Is the grant or corporation likely to support my project?
Am I, or is my project, a good candidate for the grant or donation?
What must I do to be considered?

Trust us, you will come up with dozens of potential sources and you will not have the time to apply to all of them. So, ask yourself the three questions we present and limit your focus. The third question is very important; target grants or corporate donors that require an application that you will be able to do well, given your other responsibilities and time constraints.

We suggest identifying five potential funding sources because that is a realistic number; you can always do another search later on if you have the time or the need for more funding. After you write them down, prioritize them and decide which application you will start first. Note that for many corporate donors, especially those that you identify based on shared interests, a letter outlining your project will suffice. In fact, the solicitation letter we discuss early in this book can probably be revised and used. With grants, however, there most always is a specific form for your proposal, or an application, and not following directions may disqualify you from consideration.

That leads us to our next point. After you identify the funding source you will focus on first, work only on that application until it is submitted. If you try to work on too many at once, you are more likely to make a mistake or not finish any one at all. So, your next task is to print out the instructions for the grant application and check off each part of the application as you complete it. Here it is difficult to give you advice because each application will be different. In the "Resources" chapter of this book, we have included an example of a grant application and a corporate solicitation letter for your reference. Common to most grant applications, as well as a good corporate solicitation letter, are the following points:

a detailed explanation of your project
the timeline for completion
progress to date
people or programs that are supervising your work
how your project meets the grant's goals or expectations.

The most important advice we can give you is to make sure you follow the directions and guidelines exactly. Give the funders what they want; it's the least you can do for the chunk of money you could receive and it will ensure that you have the best chance to get what you are after. The next most important advice is to prepare a cover letter for your application (unless you are expressly told not to do so). This will let you personalize your application a bit. Also in the "Resources" chapter of this book, we have included one for your review. Of course, if your "proposal" is in letter form, as with a corporate solicitation, there is no need to write a separate cover letter.

Some grants also require accountability and progress reporting, though smaller grants may not. Again, make sure you are familiar with all of the requirements, both so that you can determine at the start if a particular grant will work for you, as well as to be in compliance if you are lucky enough to get an award. Once you apply for a grant or corporate donation, record that in your notebook. You may want to use the following format:

Funding source:
Contact information:
Name of grant (if different):
Date submitted or mailed:
Do I need to follow-up on the application:
Date of follow-up:
Outcome of application:
Do I have to file anything after I receive the grant:
If so, what and when:
If so, date completed:

The largest grant we received was $1,000. It came from People to People and we were eligible to apply for it as a member youth group (yet another good reason to form a Chapter). We also arranged a matching grant, which meant that if we secured a grant from one source, another source agreed to match it. That second source for us was a private donor. The idea of a matching grant works well because donors often want to know that you are working as hard as possible to arrange funding for your project. If you search "matching grants" you will come up with some sources; otherwise, you can approach any potential donor and pitch the idea of a matching grant arrangement. Sometimes a grant you apply for will require you to set up a matching grant in order to be eligible for funding from it. Here is an important point: if you have an active youth group, you can make your youth group the source for a matching grant and then create a fundraising project within it to meet the grant requirements.

So, here are a few final words on seeking grants. Be clear. Mold the explanation of your project to fit the purpose of the grant. Be as careful filling out the grant application as you would be if you were filling out a college application. Make sure you follow directions. Be proud of what you are doing and express that. And, if you are rejected, consider revising your proposal and resubmitting it. On this last point, grant funders will sometimes tell you why you did not get the funding or where your application failed. If this is the case, fix it! It will be easier to do a revision than to start a new application (although all those after the first will be easier), so the time is well spent. And stick with the idea of applying. There is a lot of funding out there and some of it is waiting for you!

And now we have saved perhaps the most important point about grants for last. Deadlines. Most grant applications have deadlines and, as with most other things in life to which deadlines apply, not paying attention to them will disqualify your application. So, as you are considering grants, make sure you highlight any deadlines that you need to be aware of and then meet them. As you are considering different grant possibilities, you should also consider whether deadlines will work for your project and any other commitments you may have to focus on. Deadlines can mean the difference between getting funding or not.

8

Shout It From The Rooftops

*E*arlier we talked about casting a wide net as you seek support for your project. In this chapter, we talk about the importance of publicizing your work. Basically, here we are talking about personally telling as many people as you possibly can about what you are doing and using the press as an important tool.

Here are a few examples of how communicating widely about our project made a great difference.

In one instance, we told a woman who is a friend of our mom what we were trying to accomplish and she thought it was a great idea. She was in education and mentioned that schools within the New York City public school system run an annual "Penny Harvest" campaign to collect money for charities. We did some research and, with her help, contacted schools that were involved in this project. We then pitched the idea through our letter and got donations of several hundred dollars annually for about three years. In another instance, we were referred to a group within our aunt's workplace that was in charge each year of running a collection and identifying various charities that would receive the donations. We sent the head of that group our letter and received a check within a few months.

Here's another example of how talking to people about your project pays off. As we said earlier, in an effort to be creative in looking for donors for our school project, we tried to think of people and groups that shared our interest in education. We contacted a group of tutors since they are mostly educators and make a good deal of money from education. We asked them for donations from the money they make tutoring. Some gave us a percentage of what they made in a day, while others gave a percentage of what they made in a week or even a month. A few even agreed to forego any compensation for a day and gave us all of the money they charged their students.

There are so many more examples that we could give you. We already mentioned the young girl who donated $500 when she heard what we were doing. Or the people we met on a trip we took who each made substantial donations after hearing us talk about our goals. The value of telling people, and having those people tell people, cannot be overstated. We still are talking about The Hopeful School to this day and, still, that conversation generates interest. Word of mouth was as important as any one of our other fundraising ideas.

While word of mouth is largely a one-on-one endeavor, you also need to spread the news of your project widely. To do this, take advantage of free advertising through the newspapers in your area. Now, you need to realize that the likelihood of convincing *The New York Times* to run an article about your project is small, actually pretty much nonexistent. But, community newspapers love to write about local kids doing good things. So, this is one of the best routes you will find to publicize your work.

Remember that the point here is not to get publicity for yourself. It is to get word out about what you are doing so you can attract more supporters. If 1,000 people read a community newspaper that is circulated through five towns, that is an amazing opportunity to pitch your cause to a lot of potential donors. One newspaper article reached as many people as our first mailing! And, yes, a good deal of money and even some calls and letters of support came in from that exposure.

We had actually used the press well before the school project. We used it to sell our solar flashlights, to collect thousands of books, to gather winter clothes and canned goods, and to generate support for all of the activities we ran through our youth group before the Uganda school project began. The key to using the press is to make it as easy as possible for them to give you the publicity you want. By this we mean that you have a far greater chance of getting press space if you provide a well-written article that requires little work on their part. If you supply artwork, such as photos, they love that too. So, we got the address of the newspaper from the page that features letters to the editor and prepared our articles and photos, and drafted a short cover letter. We also made a point of submitting material on a regular basis. There was not one time that the newspaper did not print our submissions. And the publicity that generated was a huge boost for our project.

Newspapers are not the only "press" that you can use to publicize your project. Magazines, particularly those associated with your school, are another good resource. For example, our high school published a glossy magazine twice a year highlighting student accomplishments, along with fundraising events. It was sent to every current family, as well as graduates and faculty. We spoke to the man who was responsible for putting the magazine together and he offered to include an article on our project in one of the issues. From that, we not only got donations, but some people referred us to other funding sources, as well.

In the "Resources" chapter at the back of this book, there is a sample article and cover letter. Remember, the more people who know about your project, the more successful it will be. Getting free publicity from mass media is the best way to reach hundreds, or even thousands, of people with no cost to you and very little effort.

9

About Accountability

*H*ave your parents or teachers ever told you that you are accountable for your actions? Well, that's true. From the time we are really young we are held accountable for what we do. Now, ask someone for money and accountability takes on huge importance! If you are not accountable, one of two things will happen to your project. Either you will not get money in the first place or you will get money once and then never again.

Accountability begins as soon as you start soliciting support for what you are doing. When you approach an organization proposing to do something that will benefit it, like we did, the first thing you will need to explain is how you will be responsible in handling the project and representing the cause that you are focusing on. If you don't have a well-thought-out plan and a clearly defined goal and method for accomplishing it, some organizations may not be interested in having you represent them.

Accountability begins with researching the cause you want to undertake. It not only will impress the sponsor that you did your homework and know what the organization or cause you have chosen is all about, but it will also help you in seeking support from potential donors. This last point is very important. Being well-versed in the nature of what you want to accomplish and how you plan to go about it may be the difference between a donation and not. This applies to all types of donations, but especially money. You need to realize that even those people parting only with five or ten dollars may still want to know where the money is going and how it will be used. Think about what people say about giving money to beggars on the street. There we are talking about a dollar, or spare change, yet the potential "donors" often look the other way, refusing to give money to what they believe could be a negative cause, like funding a drug or alcohol habit. Now keep that in mind and think about asking people for bigger donations. People don't want to throw away money that they have worked hard to earn.

Here is an example about one of our bigger donors who also happened to be the most demanding about accountability before he wrote his check. This person is a very successful businessman who worked his way up from humble beginnings. He gives a good deal of money each year to charities, but is incredibly careful in deciding what he will support. We sent him our solicitation letter and then followed up with a telephone call because we knew of his reputation for donating generously to charitable causes. He said he wanted to have a telephone conference with both of us to discuss our request and the project that his money would benefit. He made a point of letting us know that he wanted to give us time to prepare our pitch and was interested in how well we would do with convincing him to make a donation. We were, of course, very familiar with our project, but did some more research on Fields of Growth and Coach Dugan. We wanted to have very specific answers to his questions about the organization that would be receiving his money and its leadership. We even called Coach Dugan to ask if there was anything we should know that might concern our potential donor regarding the organization and its work in Uganda. We also wanted more specific information about the phases of the construction and the timeline.

We made some notes for our conference and also decided who of us would have what responsibility during the discussion. Our potential donor made it very clear that he was investing time from his busy schedule to understand this project that we were asking him to support. We made it clear to ourselves that we needed to take his interest seriously and be organized enough to convince him that his money would not go to waste.

We had arranged the conference according to our schedules so that we would be in a quiet place and not be rushed. When the time came, we called him and began by repeating that we were working to build a permanent school in Uganda to replace a facility made of mud, cloth and paper. He stopped us and said that he had read our letter and wanted to talk about things that it did not cover. So, we tried to not get flustered and asked him what questions he would like us to address. He wanted to know how we came up with the idea for the project and how well we knew Fields of Growth and Coach Dugan. It became obvious to us that what he really wanted to know was if his money would be spent as we represented and that it would be useful in bringing about some positive change. It was very important to him that our project was realistic, that we were working with people who could be trusted to do what we said would be done, and that we were accountable and responsible for ensuring that the money would get where it was supposed to go and be used as promised. For example, he asked, "How do you know that when you send someone my check, that person will not just use it for himself or for some purpose none of us have considered?" That's a good question, right? Well, the only way to address that was for us to explain the past work that Coach Dugan and Fields of Growth had done in Uganda and the progress that had already been made on the project. What he was really asking about was accountability.

We also found it useful to explain to him some specifics about our fundraising. We told him how much we had collected so far, the types of donor support we had gotten, how we recorded the donations, and how we forwarded them to Fields of Growth.

We also talked about what Fields of Growth did with the money once it received it, how the money specifically was being spent, how the project was being conducted, and what phase of construction future funding would support.

In the end, he gave us a large donation. In fact, he said he would have given us more, but we caught him late in the year and he had already done most of his charitable giving. He said he would consider giving us additional funds as the project progressed and you can be sure we made a note of that and followed-up the next year.

Now we are using the term "accountability" in a broad sense here. This last example we gave you shows that accountability required us to know our project and to be available to discuss it and answer questions. For us, that made the difference between getting a big donation and not. Accountability, though, also includes what you do after you convince someone to give you a donation. We have already talked about keeping good records of what you collect and promptly getting it to the charity that is benefitting from your work. Sure, that is accountability; but accountability also means that you must be willing to make those records available to any donor, or parent organization, or beneficiary organization that wants to see them. With our project, no one actually asked to see our records, but if they had, we would have been able to provide that information on the spot.

Another aspect of accountability is following up with your donors. A "thank you" note acknowledging the donation is critical. Make sure you are sincere and get it out as soon as you receive the contribution to your project. We had some of the kids from Uganda write a letter in English about their hopes and dreams and decorate the border. On the back, we handwrote a "thank you" note to our donors in black pen, leaving blank the date and the donor's name. We then made two-sided color copies that were a good quality, so they looked original. The text of our "thank you" letter is in the "Resources" chapter at the end of this book. When we got a donation in, we used the same black pen to write in the date, the donor's name and sign our names, then we mailed it out. This way of acknowledging donations was really well-thought-out. By using the letter from one of the children who would benefit from the school, we were able to give our donors another indication of where their money was going and whom it would benefit. By photocopying the letter and creating a prototype for the "thank you" note, we saved ourselves a lot of time. By handwriting the note and personalizing it, we hoped to make donors feel more of a connection to us and our work and hoped to convey how sincere we were in thanking them. Mailing the letter, rather than emailing it, was also a more personal touch and provided a greater likelihood of receipt. The one thing we did not do, but which you could easily include, would be to list the amount of the donation in each letter. This would provide the donor with a receipt for tax purposes. Of course, for donations that are received in the form of checks, the cashed check serves as the receipt. We also made sure that we included in our solicitation letter, notice that the donation would be tax deductible.

Now, there are a lot of people who will not get a thank you note. All the ones who buy your doughnuts or put spare change into your water bottles in all likelihood will not get a personal, written acknowledgement. And when an organization supports your project, like the Penny Harvest campaign within the New York City schools, you will send one "thank you" that applies to the many people who participated. That can be sent to whomever your contact person was, with the hope that he or she will share it with the others. The important point is to show your thanks and to express that as often as you practically can. We have given you an example of how we did it, but there are many other ways. Just make sure that you find one way you are comfortable with and stay on top of it.

The last comment that we want to make about accountability also relates to following up. Many times, once people get a donation and acknowledge it, that is their last contact with the donor. That's fine for most donors; most people do not expect any follow-up thereafter. It's a nice touch, though, when people have supported the project you are involved with, to let them know your progress. Toward that end, we added a line in our solicitation letter that told people to give us their email address if they would like periodic updates on the project. This is a simple enough thing to do and it really is your donor's right to know how the project is coming along. This goes directly back to the type of accountability that the large donor who questioned us was talking about. By giving people progress reports, you let them know that their donation is working and you bring them closer to your cause. In a few instances, we even got repeat donations when we reported that a certain phase of the project was done and we were collecting for the next stage.

The service project you hopefully will choose to do after you read this book may be your first and last, or it may be the beginning of a lifetime commitment to service. Whichever is the case, you only help yourself by making accountability a central focus of your effort. It's not only something you do for your donors; it makes you look good and will generate enthusiasm for your work and support for future projects if that is the direction you choose to take.

10

Are You Really Done?

Some projects have a natural and obvious ending point. If you are collecting for a Thanksgiving food collection, you know you will be done by Thanksgiving. The same was true of our holiday book drive; by the second week in December our books were collected, sorted and distributed and the project was over. On the other hand, if you are selling solar flashlights to generate matching donations, your project can go on forever. You actually are the one who will decide when your project is done.

If you really want to get philosophical, you can stare at the clouds and think about how much need there is in the world and how one can never truly be done with service. But, that is not the approach we are taking here. What we are talking about is sitting down with yourself at a point when you think your project could be over and evaluating how it went and whether there is more that you want to do.

Trying to objectively evaluate how your project went is basically a survey of what you did right and what you did wrong. Don't rush this part; it's a really valuable exercise, particularly if you plan to do another project at any time in the future. In fact, it's so important that you should make yourself write some notes on the experience while it is fresh in your mind. Think about what worked and what did not work so well. Think about things you would change the next time. Think about ideas that came to you too late, but that you would have wanted to try. By writing it down in your project notebook, you can look back on it either for yourself or to give advice to someone else who is undertaking a project in the future. Ask yourself the tough question of whether you are happy with what you did and satisfied that you gave the project all the effort it deserved or needed. And, if the answer is no, still pat yourself on the back for giving it a shot and resolve to try a little harder the next time you decide to do something that is important to you or someone else.

Now, be prepared for the possibility that once you sit down to evaluate how your project went, you may come to the conclusion that there is still more you can or want to accomplish. For us, when we reached the point that the new school was built and was operating, we realized that we had accomplished our goal. We also realized that we could have walked away at that point and felt really satisfied. After all, after much effort and creativity, the kids at The Hopeful School had a far better environment in which to learn and grow. We had achieved what we set out to do. Yet, we realized that just because we could cross off of our list the project to build a permanent school in Uganda, there was more that could be accomplished. For example, the school could have better furnishings. Textbooks and school supplies were limited, at best. The uniforms the kids wore were mismatched and tattered, while their feet were always bare and covered with mud.

Once at a fundraiser, Coach Dugan said that the worst thing you can do is show up in these villages and give the people hope, then disappear. That kept ringing in our ears and his voice still is heard. It's likely that no one would have blamed us if we put away our files and said we were done, since we accomplished what we had set out to do. Funding a new school in an African village is not a small feat. But, obvious need still exists there. So, we decided that stage two of our school project, whenever we could undertake it, would be to try to find corporate sponsors to supply things like books, paper, computers, printers, desks, uniforms, etc. This would take on a very different character than our construction effort, however.

The reason this second phase would be different was because our situation was changing. The point here is to be realistic about evaluating what you will take on and the time frame for completing it. It's important to consider that what you could do at one stage of your life, in one environment, may not be possible when circumstances change. For us, we were heading off to college in different cities. That meant we would not have the same time available that we had gotten used to having, and that working together from different locations would be more difficult. To accommodate our changed circumstances, we would have to modify our approach. First, our time frame for reaching our goal of securing sponsors for the school had to be very loose; we had to be realistic about the time we could devote to a new venture while we were experiencing an important and very different stage of our lives. The fact was that the school was functioning and the students were happy and learning, so there was not the urgency we felt when we were raising money to build the physical structure itself. We also talked about targeting only corporate sponsors. This was based on the fact that we had asked just about everyone we ever met for money for the school construction project. In addition, solicitation that targets individuals is more time-consuming and generally brings in smaller donations. It made most sense when we got to the point of thinking about this second phase, to target donors who could make a big difference by way of a single solicitation.

Phase two is still mostly just a plan. But, it came from the fact that when we asked ourselves if we were done, the answer was "yes" and "no." Yes, our first project was finished and we had succeeded in achieving our goal. The Hopeful School was a reality. Yet, we also recognized that there is more that we could do. We would have to approach it differently and tailor it to what our schedules allowed in this next stage of life, but we would keep our eyes on that service-related goal.

11

A Word About College Applications

deally, you will get involved in service because you want to, not because someone has told you it will look good on a college application. The reality is that most American high school students do believe, and rightly so, that in addition to good grades, good SAT/ACT scores, good extracurricular activities, and a good essay, they need to be able to show some service on their resumes or college applications. While that does paint a picture of well-roundedness that the colleges seem to want to see, be careful about what you choose to do and how you spend your "service" hours.

Our very unscientific research indicates that it is probably impossible to find a college junior without some service credit. Schools require it and some even chart each student's progress for service awards like the one given out by the President of the United States for service hours that meet certain thresholds. There are also those helicopter parents who search out service opportunities for their kids and drag them into service while cheerfully proclaiming that their children are only too happy to get involved.

Counting on service in a general or generic sense to get you into college is a mistake. Colleges tend to see through a forced dabble in service, as opposed to a genuine commitment and an experience that makes a meaningful difference. How do we know that? We will tell you what we learned in the college admissions process.

On our college applications, we each listed various service activities through our school, through People to People, and through our youth group which we formed before we were even in middle school. On a number of our acceptance letters, admissions heads wrote personal notes to us. Those notes congratulated us for our service activity, but not the "routine" involvement that was common to most other applicants. Instead, the letters focused on our project to build a school in Uganda. That is what caught their attention and distinguished our volunteer work from the volunteer work of hundreds of thousands of applicants across America. So, we wanted to find out why.

We spoke to the admissions people who had specifically commented on our Uganda project. In one instance, we had the opportunity to speak in person with the admissions representative who wrote us a note. He explained that "service" is the hot word in college applications these days. He said that virtually every applicant has gotten service experience, whether on a trip his or her parents paid for over a school break or through projects orchestrated by one's high school. He had seen literally thousands of youth programs and church-affiliated service groups and his comment about them all was, "We see through the veneer. We know what is real service activity and the run-of-the-mill stuff that every kid is encouraged to do by a parent or guidance counselor. What we are interested in, and see far less frequently, is a sustained commitment to service and involvement that shows leadership. That is where your project to build a school stood out."

At an accepted student day at another university known for its limited acceptance of out-of-state students, we asked the question of what the difference was between getting in or not. The difference was, we were told, "something else." The admissions person explained that every applicant has outstanding grades, outstanding test scores, and outstanding involvement outside of classes, whether that is in music, athletics, science and technology, writing, theater or service. The challenge is for an applicant to show that he or she is different, that he or she has all that plus something else that others don't have.

Now, nothing in this chapter is meant to convince you that a week rebuilding homes after a natural disaster or a spring break trip to a developing country to work with orphans is not worthwhile. In fact, the whole purpose of this book is to encourage you to get out there and do something that will make a difference in this world. And, yes, those "run of the mill" service activities do make a difference. Things like the Presidential Service Award or other service-based distinctions do not place a value on one type of volunteer effort over another. Whenever anything you do helps someone or something, it is a worthwhile effort.

The point this chapter makes is that if you are inclined to do service work solely in order to get into the college you hope to attend, you may be disappointed. Apart from the randomness of the college acceptance game, service must be something that is truly out of the ordinary in order to drive your admission decision (or scholarship money). Now, understand that "out of the ordinary" may mean funding a school or simply starting a youth group that endures and shows your sustained commitment to service over a period of years. Basically, if you are motivated, even in part, by the college admissions process, then whatever you pursue should demonstrate your creativity, leadership and dedication.

So, what can you do with that information? Well, you can do the more "standard" service activities that are set-up for you and know that while that will contribute to your overall profile as an applicant, it will not have a significant impact on whether you will be accepted or not. Or, you can come up with your own project and take on something that is unique and substantial and that will distinguish you as an innovator and a leader. That is how you will set yourself apart from others, if some of your motivation for engaging in service is to do that. And this book is your blueprint to service projects that will allow you to stand out from the crowd.

One last word here about your motivation to get involved with service. We didn't decide to build the school in Uganda because we thought it would look good on a college application. When we got involved in the Uganda project, or even started our youth group, it was well before anyone was thinking about college, especially us. That, too, by the way, was noted by many of the colleges that offered us admission. We came to the project out of concern for kids in Uganda who have so much less than we have. It was the same sense that made us start a youth group and collect books for the underprivileged. We wound up with college essays about our service work very much after the fact. What you should take from that is the lesson that anything you do in life that is motivated by something you truly believe in will be far more exciting and far easier to accomplish; that there might be some unexpected benefit to you as a result of doing it, is a gift.

12

Can One Person Really Make a Difference?

By now, your answer to the question, "Can one person really make a difference?" should be a resounding, "Yes!" The purpose of this book is to convince you that through service you can make a difference. Whether you work alone or as part of a group project, your effort will directly benefit someone somewhere.

In Chapter 2 we spoke about people who inspired us. Because of Coach Dugan, a village in Uganda is better and its kids are learning how to become independent as adults. The work of John Wood has contributed to the education of tens of thousands of children around the world. Bill and Melinda Gates have improved the health and welfare of people whose lives, without them, may have been lost. And we, two kids growing up in a New York City suburb, helped to give lacrosse to kids in a faraway continent and then build a school where they could learn in some degree of comfort.

Whether your act of service is to visit an elderly neighbor, or spend a Saturday at a soup kitchen, or help repair homes after a storm, or something bigger, it makes a difference to someone. Quite simply, without you a project may not get done or, at the very least, it would take longer to complete. For every act of charity, there is somewhere a recipient.

You can make a difference, so now go out and create some change!

13

Resources

The pages which follow are intended to help you through the various stages of your project. Some pages serve as examples of material we produced and used in our own service, while others provide references to valuable Internet sites and other resources.

Resource Index

Forming A People to People Chapter

When we refer in this book to our youth group, we are speaking about a charitable organization we formed as a local chapter of People to People. You should be aware that People to People also runs national and international "Global Youth Forums," which are trips that chapter members can register for and attend. The parent organization often offers scholarships which students can apply for to offset the program costs.

As we explained earlier in this book, we started our chapter of People to People soon after we created our youth group so that we could organize ourselves around an organization that people would recognize and that would offer to our members a variety of other opportunities. Chapters are groups of 10 or more students, with one or two parent advisors, which carry out People to People's mission of peace through understanding on a local level. We viewed that mission to have a central core of charity and service, and organized ourselves around that. You may recruit members for your chapter and are likely to also receive referrals from People to People of students who are looking to get involved in their community. Once you form a chapter, your group is eligible for grants and awards. People to People will also give you project ideas if you need some help in that area.

Chapters are classified as "Student Chapters" for people in high schools, colleges and/or universities or as "Community Chapters" for families and people of all ages. Ours was a Student Chapter. To start a Student Chapter there are six initial steps:

Submit a membership list of at least 10 people
Hold a meeting to elect officers and plan at least four projects for the year
Submit a project planning form
Read and sign the Student Chapter Bylaws
Submit a Student Chapter Charter Application
Identify at least one adult advisor

You can view all of those forms and get more information at *chapters@ ptpi.org*. As you review that information, be aware that there are other requirements, such as collecting dues and filing reports of your chapter's activities. The website has an FAQ page that should give you all of the information you need to get started.

Finding Charities to Work With

There will no doubt be some charities that you, and your members if you form a youth group to carry out your projects, come up with on your own. They may be local, national or international. They may be causes that you hear about from speaking with someone or ones that you read about or see featured on television or through social media. The following list presents some of our favorite charities, in case you need a few ideas to get you started with service:

Room to Read
Fields of Growth
Heifer International
St. Jude.org
American Cancer Society
Local soup kitchens or homeless shelters
National Red Cross
Ronald McDonald House
Action Against Hunger
Feeding America
Literacy Volunteers of America
Save the Children
The United Nations Children's Fund
Samaritan Purse
World Wildlife Fund
BoGo Solar Flashlight Partnership Program
Greenpeace

Keep in mind that you can also search the Internet by terms such as "best children's charities," "charities devoted to the environment," "charities to feed the hungry," etc. If you want to perform service for a local charity, refine your search by identifying your community along with your area(s) of interest.

Sample Individual Solicitation Letter

Dear Friends:

We are high school students, and brothers, from Manhasset, New York, who are trying to make a dream come true. The dream is not only ours; it belongs to children in Uganda and others here in America who are dedicated to improving the lives of young people in a place much less fortunate than where we live.

The dream is to build a school.

Last year, we became aware of a charity called Fields of Growth International. It is run by people who, like us, love lacrosse and want to share their passion to simply make kids happy and get them involved in an activity which can help keep them safe, healthy and change their lives. This past year we have been helping to collect used lacrosse equipment which is then shipped to Uganda. Fields of Growth uses lacrosse to foster friendship, education and human development. The basic belief of the organization is that change begins with passion and enthusiasm for anything that is a positive influence in your life. Part of the charity's mission has also been to turn fields of ruin into fields of growth and create clean, safe space where children can play.

We recently learned that $20,000 U.S. could build a school in Uganda. The school would teach kids not only basic math, reading and writing, but vocational skills which would help them grow into adults who can support themselves and their society.

So, we are asking for your help. Our dream is to raise the money for this school. Your donation, no matter how big or small, will simply help the lives of children and give them a glimpse of the opportunity that so many young people here in America take for granted.

Please donate in the name of those people or things that bring you joy!

Donations can be in cash or by check made out to **Fields of**

Growth International, with the memo "School Project," and sent c/o **Kent and Grant Schietinger, [address].** You can visit Fields of Growth International at www.fieldsofgrowthintl.com or call either of us at [telephone number] for more information. If you fill out the form below, we'll keep you advised of our progress.

Please pass this letter along to anyone who might want to help. Thank you!

Name:
Address:
Donation Amount:
Email Address:
Fields of Growth is a nonprofit organization and your gift is tax deductible.

. . . .

Remember to sign the letter. It's also a good idea to have an adult read it before you send it out, as well as someone from the charity you are highlighting. We added pictures of the school and the children, and got permission to use Fields of Growth letterhead.

Sample Corporate Solicitation Letter

Dear Sir or Madam:

We are writing to ask your company's support for a project we have undertaken which we believe would be of interest to your corporation's charitable mission.

We are high school students, and brothers, from Manhasset, New York, who are trying to make a dream come true. The dream is not only ours; it belongs to children in Uganda and others here in America who are dedicated to improving the lives of young people in a place much less fortunate than where we live.

The dream is to build a school.

Last year, we became aware of a charity called Fields of Growth International.

We recently learned that $20,000 U.S. could build a school in Uganda. The school would teach kids not only basic math, reading and writing, but vocational skills which would help them grow into adults who can support themselves and their society.

So, we are asking your company for its support. Our dream is to raise the money for this school. Your donation, no matter how big or small, will simply help the lives of children and give them a glimpse of the opportunity that so many young people here in America take for granted.

Check donations should be made out to **Fields of Growth International,** with the memo "School Project," and be sent c/o **Kent and Grant Schietinger, [address].** You can visit Fields of Growth International at www.fieldsofgrowthintl.com or contact us at **[telephone number]** or **[email address]** for more information. If your company offers a matching grant incentive, please advise us of that and we will provide you with information about our fundraising to date.

If you are not the correct person to receive this solicitation, please forward it accordingly.

Thank you, in advance, for your kind consideration.

Very truly yours,

[Your name]

. . . .

For the corporate solicitation, make sure you do your homework first. Here we provide you with a fairly generic letter. As you research potential corporate donors, you should be able to identify those whose interests align with your project. You also most likely will be able to determine, in advance, if the company offers a matching grant program, which means they match whatever amount (usually up to a limit) that you raise from other sources. Remember to have your letter proofed and approved by any specific charity you mention as the recipient.

List of Grant Sources

Remember that grants are non-repayable funds provided by one party, often a government department, corporation, foundation or trust, to a recipient that is usually a nonprofit entity, educational institution, business, group or an individual. Grants can come from the federal government, the state government, a college or career school, or a private or nonprofit organization. Do your research well and then apply for any grants that your project might be eligible for. Be sure to meet application deadlines!

This list below is a representative sample of some grant sources. You can begin with these or undertake an Internet search using terms such as "charitable grants," "grants for educational charities" (or whatever other charity you are collecting for), "matching grants," etc. Use your imagination!

Vanguard Charitable
Walmart Foundation
Bank of America
The Melinda and Bill Gates Foundation
Ronald McDonald House Charities
People to People

One very helpful Internet site is prattlibrary.org which has a directory of approximately 120,000 U.S. foundation and corporate giving programs which you can search by the grant provider's name, location, geographic focus, type of support and subjects.

The Catalog of Federal Domestic Assistance lists all U.S. government grants provided to various recipients, including nonprofit organizations.

Gov.grant is an easy-to-use source to locate available grants and provides a list of recent recipients. It also allows you to sign up to receive notices of funding opportunities through email.

Sample Grant Application

Each grant source has a different process for applying. The complexity or simplicity of a grant application may determine what you do and do not apply for. Here we are providing a relatively simple grant application to give you an idea of what type of information you may be asked for. When it comes to applying for any grant, the two most important pieces of advice we can give you are to complete the application thoroughly and thoughtfully. There is a lot of competition for funding. After that, the most important thing is to make sure you meet any deadlines that the grant provider has set.

Name:_____

Organization:_____

Project Name:_____

Project Location:_____

Date project began:_____

Expected Completion Date (if known):_____

Identify the focus of your project:_____

Describe the project in detail (use additional pages, if necessary):

_____

_____

_____

Who are the intended beneficiaries?_____

How will the project be carried out?_____

In what way will the project make a significant impact?_____

_____

What grants, if any, have you received in the past three years?

_____

_____

Project Budget (itemize in an attached sheet)

Project Financing (itemize in an attached sheet)

Sample Grant Cover Letter

Some simple grants, like those awarded by People to People, will not require anything other than the application to be filed. Others will require a cover letter to accompany an application. Where that is the case, something as simple as the following sample can be used:

Dear Sir or Madam [or grant administrator's name, if known]:

I am writing on behalf of [project name, project description or youth group] to apply for a grant through your organization. The project which I seek funding for is [provide brief description]. My position with respect to the project is [describe your role]. Attached is the completed application that is provided online.

Thank you for your consideration of this request for funding. If you require any additional information, I can be reached at [telephone number] or [email].

Very truly yours,

✿ ✿ ✿ ✿ ✿ ✿

Before you jump into the cover letter, make sure that it is something that the grant provider wants. In fact, once you find funding sources that match your project, learn more about how you should approach them. This is called the "initial contact." The initial contact can be made by direct application, telephone call, email or mail, or letter of intent (also referred to as "LOI"). The LOI is usually used for more involved grant applications where there are several steps to the process and often follows an introductory phone call. It is far more detailed than the sample transmittal letter presented above and can be thought of as a bridge between the initial contact and the formal application.

Whatever you do, just make sure you give the grant provider whatever is listed in its published guidelines.

There are many online tutorials on grant writing and applications. Look at the GrantSpace.com website or search "How to write a grant proposal."

Sample Cover Letter to Newspaper

One of this book's chapters discusses the importance of publicizing your project and tells you that local newspapers are great sources of free advertising. If you look at the editorial page of any newspaper, there is usually an email or mailing address to which correspondence can be sent. If you don't see that, then do an online search of the newspaper to find out how articles of community interest can be submitted. The following is a simple transmittal letter that requests that an article you have written be published:

Dear Sir or Madam [or name of editor, if available]:

I am a local high school student attending [name of school]. I am involved in a service project to [briefly describe project]. I have attached for your review and publication an article which describes this project and seeks community support for it. Please feel free to edit it as you like.

[If artwork is provided, note that and identify the name of the person who created it.]

I would appreciate your consideration. If you require any additional information, I can be reached at [telephone number] or [email].

Thank you for your time and assistance.

Very truly yours,

[Your Name]

Sample Newspaper Article

A local youth group headed by two high school juniors is engaged in a number of service projects to benefit the needy, both near home and abroad.

Manhasset Students For Change, chartered under the national nonprofit organization known as People to People, was founded by two brothers, Kent and Grant Schietinger of Manhasset, in 2008. Its 20 members are dedicated to service directed to the needs of families in our local community, as well as New York City and as far away as Africa. Two current projects need your support.

Throughout the month of November, the youth group is conducting a winter clothing drive to benefit St. Michael's Parish, which runs a soup kitchen located in New York's upper west side. Donations of clean coats, sweaters, pants, socks, boots, gloves, hats and scarves in good condition are requested. Donation bins are located at the library and both elementary schools. Pick-ups can also be arranged by emailing the youth group at [insert email address].

A longer-term project is a fundraising campaign to benefit a school in Uganda. This project has been ongoing for four years and has a goal of raising $20,000 to finance the construction of a permanent school to replace the current facility which is made of mud, cardboard and cloth. The school serves approximately 250 children, many of whom are orphans. The school is operated by Fields of Growth Intl., which was founded by University of Notre Dame graduate Kevin Dugan. A number of fundraising activities have been organized by the youth group over the past four years to fund the project. Donations by cash or check made out to Fields of Growth Intl. can be sent to Manhasset Students For Change, at P.O. Box 123, Manhasset NY 11030. Your donations, regardless of amount, will help improve the lives of children in need.

Any high school students who are interested in pursuing service opportunities through Manhasset Students For Change are urged to contact the organization.

Sample "Thank You" Letter

Dear [Name of Donor]:

Thank you for your generous donation of [insert amount] in support of the school project in Uganda. On the back of this note acknowledging your contribution is a letter from one of the students attending The Hopeful School. We send it to you so you can see where your donation is going. The temporary school these children have to work in is made of cloth, cardboard and mud. You can see pictures of the current school and the construction that you have contributed to at the Fields of Growth website at fieldsofgrowthintl.org.

Thank you for your generosity and compassion.

Very truly yours,

＊＊＊＊＊＊

We were fortunate to have the students' letters, collected as part of a pen pal program, to use for the back of our "thank you" notes. Anytime you can add a personal touch like that, it will make your donors feel more connected to your project. Even when that is not available, however, it is essential that you create a personal note to thank donors for their support. If you include in the note the specific amount of the donation, and you date your letter, the donor can keep it as a receipt for tax purposes.

Printed in the United States
By Bookmasters